A Star in my Heart

A Mother's Love that
Shines
Strong and Bright
Long After She's Gone

For every little one who
misses their Mommy
May you always feel
her love shining softly inside you,
like a star in your heart.

This book
belongs to

_____

Book Cover by Tukotuku Publishing
Illustrations by Tukotuku Publishing
First edition 2025
Print ISBN:978-1-991366-15-3
Ebook ISBN:978-1-991366-16-0

Hello, little one.
This story is for you—
especially if your Mom isn't here anymore.
Sometimes, when someone we love is gone,
our hearts feel a bit confused or heavy.
That's okay. This book is a
gentle way to help you
understand those big feelings.
Even when someone we love isn't near us
anymore, the love they gave us stays
forever—like a star that keeps glowing
inside our hearts.

My Mom isn't here anymore

and
Sometimes
that makes
my heart
feel
sad

it feels
like a
big storm
in my chest.

That's called grief...

Grief means
I loved her so much

And
I miss
her even
more

Some days my heart feels so sad that I just want to cry

Some days
I just feel like
being quiet.

My dad says
all those feelings
are okay.

He gives me
a big hug when
I feel wobbly.

I miss
her hugs.

Her
Laugh

Sometimes I think:
"Where did
Mom Go."

Some people say
she is a star in the Sky

Some say she
lives in my heart.

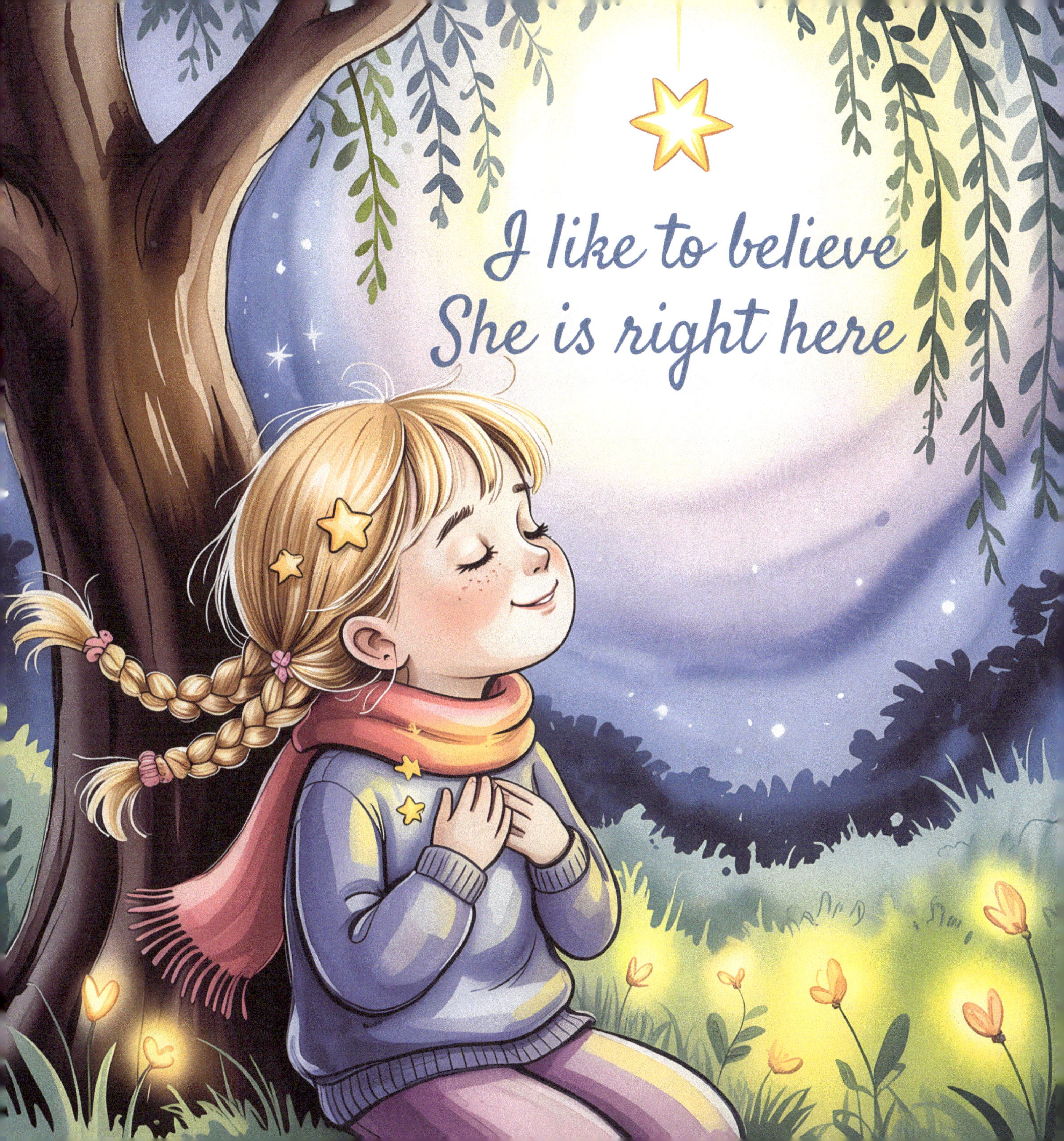

I like to believe
She is right here

With Me—
Always

We did everything together

She
was my
Everything.

But now
she's
gone

So, now
I write
to her

Every
Day

and I
tell
her

Everything that has happened that day

I even tell
her jokes

And I just know that She would Love them

Today
I decided to
do something
different

"I'm going to make a memory box"--I thought smiling.

Just for
my
Mommy,

and fill it with everything that reminds me of her.

My favorite
pictures
of her and I
together

Her
favorite
leaves and
flowers

Pictures and cards that I made just for her

Everything just for my Mommy

Even though
my Mom
has gone...

Her love
is still
here...

Her love still
lives on, in my
smiles, in my
laughter
and in my tears

Somedays
I feel sad,
and
somedays I
feel happy

But
everyday

I carry a Star
in my heart
just for my
Mom

Because Love
never really
leaves

it just
changes
shape

And even though
Mom is gone,
her love will forever
stay as a
Star in my
heart

A Note for your Heart

When someone you love — like a Mother leaves,
it can feel like your heart has a missing piece.
But little by little, as you remember the cuddles,
the playtimes, and the love you shared...
something amazing happens.
That missing piece becomes a memory,
and that memory becomes part of who you are.
Your heart grows.
And the love you gave —
and felt —
stays with you, always.
Wherever you go,
whatever you do,
your Mother's star
will walk beside you...
tucked safely in your heart.

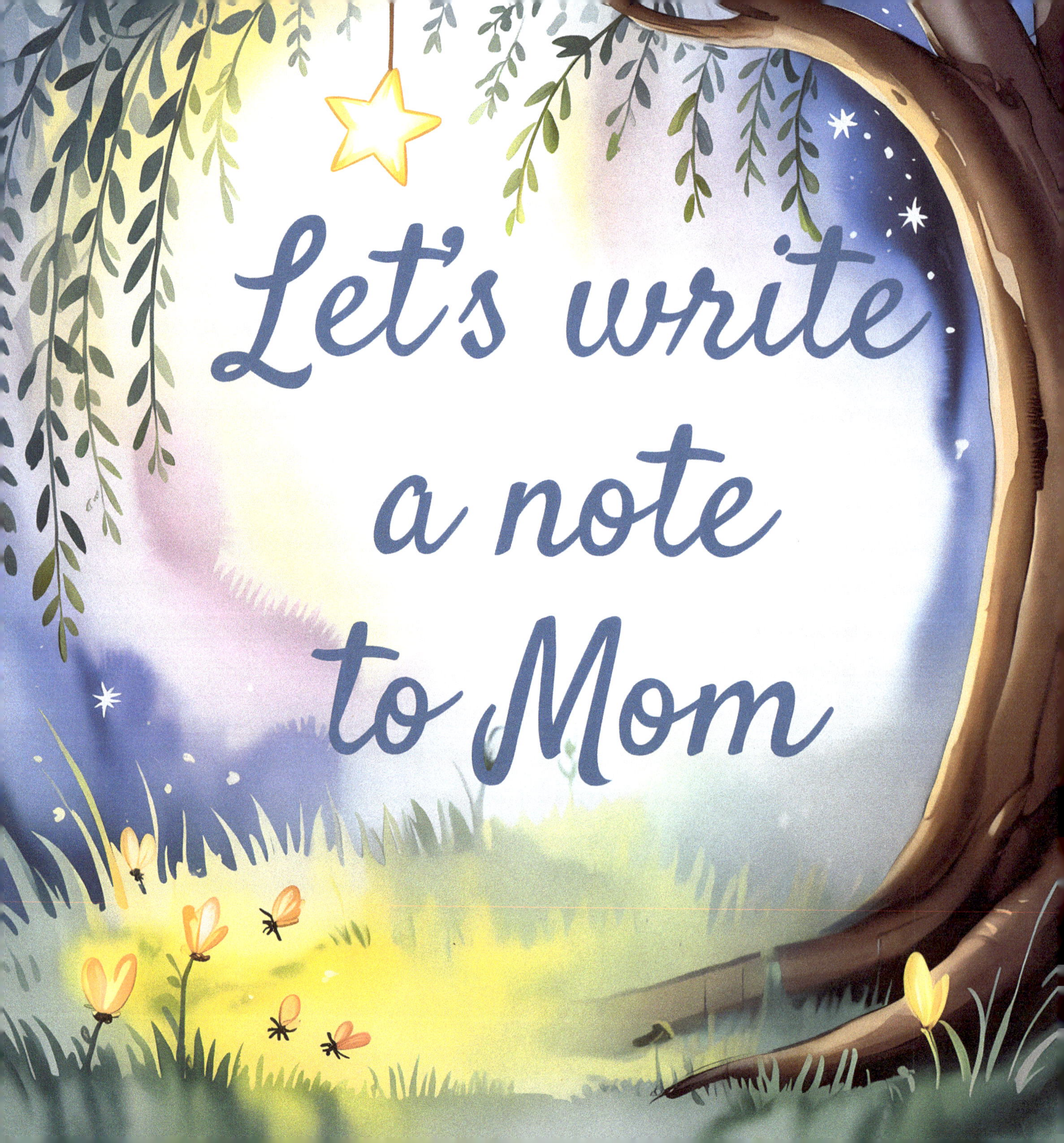
Let's write a note to Mom

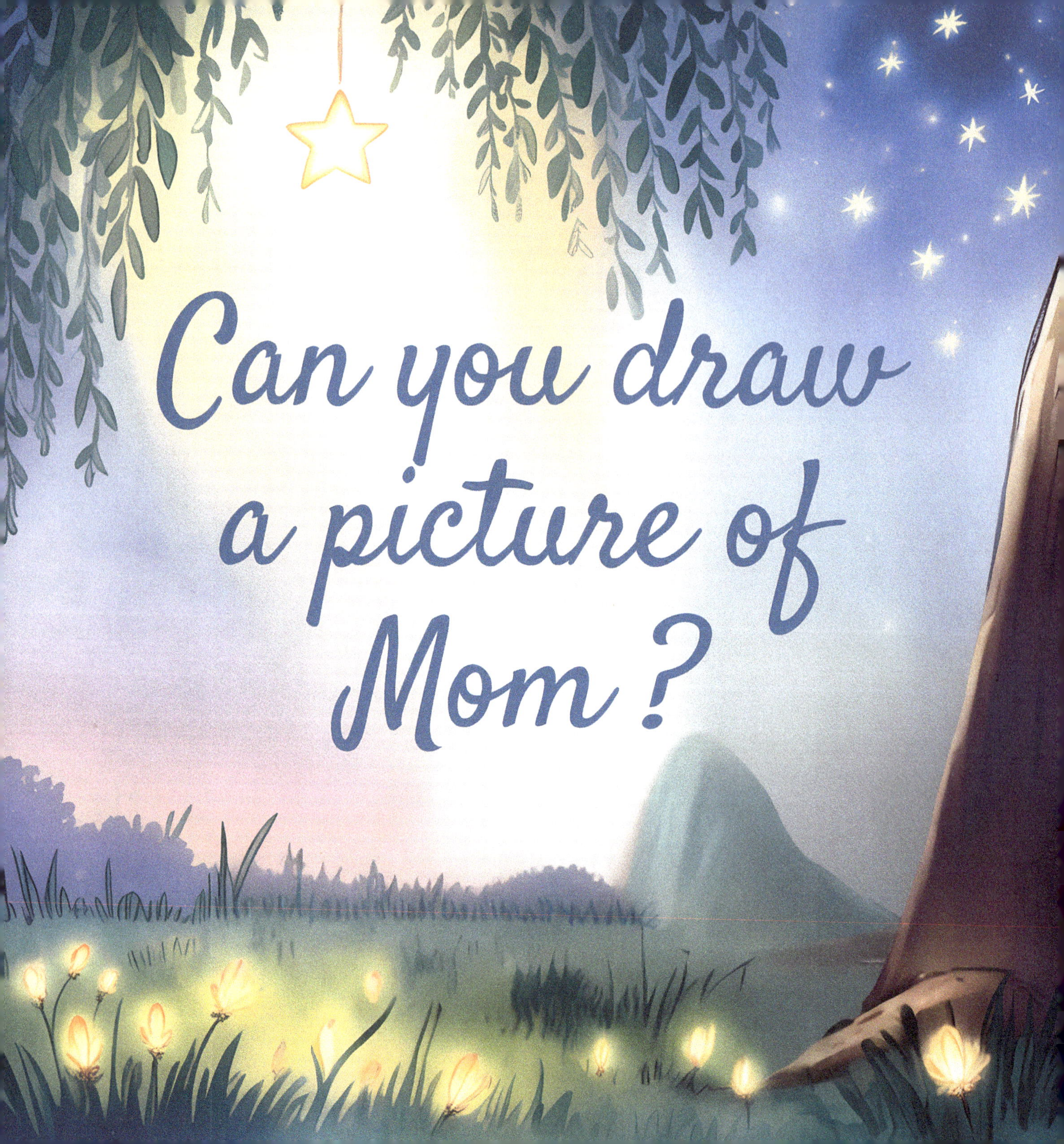

Can you draw a picture of Mom?

Can you draw
a favorite
memory that
you have

What would you like to tell Mom

Draw something
that made
Mom
different and unique

Draw a memory that makes you smile when you think of Mom

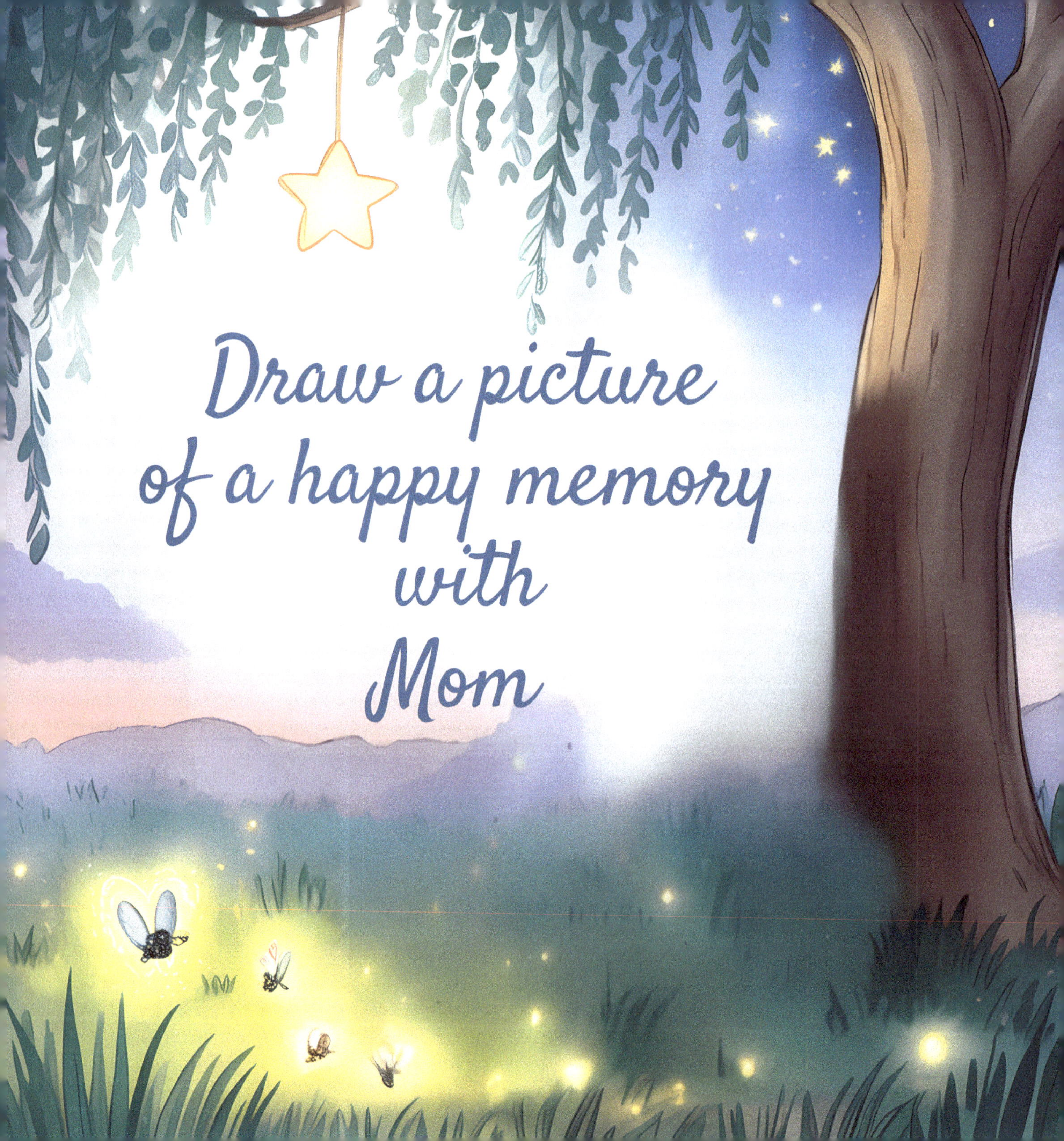
Draw a picture
of a happy memory
with
Mom

Let's create your own
story about Mom. It can
be happy, sad, funny, or
all of those.
start with
"Once Upon A Time...."

The End

A Note for Grown-Ups

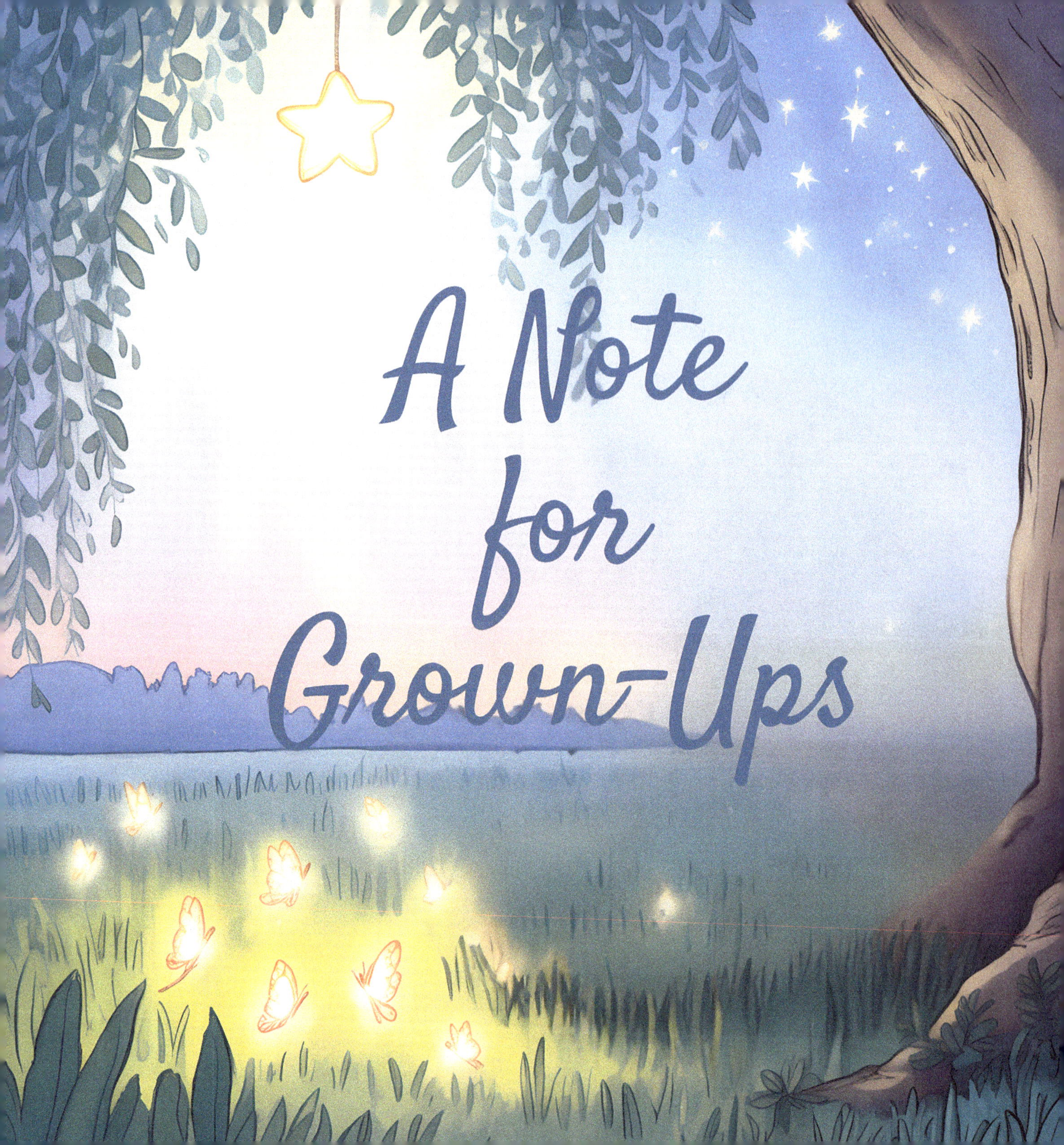

Supporting your
Child through the loss of a Mother

Losing a parent can be a child's first experience with deep grief. It can bring up big feelings—sadness, confusion, even fear. A Star in My Heart was created to gently help your child explore those emotions and begin the healing journey through love,
memories, and creativity.
Here's how you can support them along the way:
Let them talk freely about Mom and what they miss.
Encourage drawing, storytelling,
or letter writing to express feelings.
Reassure them that all emotions are okay—
there's no wrong or right way to grieve.
Share your own memories and feelings, showing that it's okay to feel and remember together.
This book is a soft space where your child can feel safe, loved, and reminded that even though Mom is gone,
her love still lives in their heart.

Validate their Feelings

Children may express sadness, anger, guilt, or even relief.
All of these are normal.
Let your child know it's okay to feel what they're feeling — and that grief doesn't have a timeline.
Say things like-
**"I miss Mommy too." Let your child know it's okay to feel sad.
"I'm here for you."**

Create Space for Expression

Encourage creative outlets-drawing,

journaling,storytelling.
or even role-playing.
Let them choose how they'd like to honor
and remember their Mom.

Talk Honestly About Death

Use age appropriate language

Avoid confusing phrases like "went to sleep" — instead, gently explain that all living beings have a life cycle.

Honest conversations build trust and emotional resilience.

Rituals
Can Help

Creating a memory box,
planting a flower,
or holding a simple ceremony
can give children
a sense of closure and a tangible
way to say goodbye.

Model Healthy Grieving

If you're grieving it's okay to show it.
When children see you
sharing your emotions openly,
it reassures them that
sadness is part of love —
not something to hide..

Most importantly,
Their Mother may be gone,
but the bond they shared will
always be part
of who they are.
with love,
Michelle

Let's meet
Michelle
Huirama

Hi! I'm Michelle, and I write gentle picture books for little ones learning about big feelings. When my own loved ones passed away, I wished there had been a soft, simple story I could read to the children in my life—something that would help them feel safe, loved, and less alone. That's why I wrote A Star in My Heart. It's a gentle hug in book form, made to help children understand grief and remember the love that never goes away.
I believe even the smallest hearts deserve stories that bring light during dark times. I hope this book brings comfort to your family and helps keep Mom's love shining bright.

Ko Tukotuku te Reikura
Ko Tamainupo te Hapu
Ko Karioi te Maunga
Ko Waikato te Ipukarea
Ko Tainui te Waka

Even if your Mom isn't here to tuck
you in or hold your hand, her love is
still with you—every single day.
It shines in your smile, your hugs,
your drawings,
and the kind things you do.
When you look up at
the stars or feel warm inside, that
might just be your Mom saying,
"I love you."
And you can say
it right back.
Because love like that
never goes away.

Written with
Empathy and Care
This story reminds families
that saying goodbye
doesn't mean forgetting...
It means remembering
with love.